Getting Through
to the Wonderful You

Getting Through to the Wonderful You

*A Christian Alternative
to Transcendental Meditation*

Charlie W. Shedd

FLEMING H. REVELL COMPANY
OLD TAPPAN, NEW JERSEY

Unless otherwise identified, Scripture references in this volume are from the King James Version of the Bible.

Scripture quotations identified MOFFATT are from THE BIBLE: A NEW TRANSLATION by James Moffatt. Copyright 1954 by James A. R. Moffatt. By permission of Harper & Row, Publishers, Inc.

Scripture quotations identified LB are from The Living Bible, Copyright © 1971 by Tyndale House Publishers, Wheaton, Illinois 60187. All rights reserved.

Scripture quotations identified RSV are from the Revised Standard Version of the Bible, copyrighted 1946, 1952, © 1971 and 1973.

Entries identified (WCD) are used by permission. From Webster's New Collegiate Dictionary © 1975 by G. & C. Merriam Co., Publishers of the Merriam-Webster Dictionaries.

Entries identified (RHD) are reprinted by permission from THE RANDOM HOUSE DICTIONARY OF THE ENGLISH LANGUAGE, © 1966, 1973 by Random House, Inc.

Entries identified (F&W) are from FUNK & WAGNALLS STANDARD COLLEGE DICTIONARY. Copyright © 1973, 1968, 1966, 1963 by Funk & Wagnalls Publishing Company, Inc., with permission of the publisher.

Library of Congress Cataloging in Publication data

Shedd, Charlie W
    Getting through to the wonderful you.

    Includes index.
    1. Prayer. 2. Meditation. 3. Devotional   exercises. I. Title.
BV210.2.S48   248'.3   75-43875
ISBN 0-8007-0780-X

To Tim
seventeen—
and wonderful

Contents

Preface

I am wonderfully made.
Psalms 139:14 LB

Thank you, psalmist, for reminding me. Sometimes I don't see how this could be.

But there it is! Like a steady note of hope, this major refrain from the Book:

Every one of us is stamped with the Divine imprint.

The purpose of this book is to describe one way of getting through to the wonderful you.

Prayer
Lord, show me what You had in mind
When You first thought of me.

Getting Through
to the Wonderful You

So God made man like his Maker.
Like God did God make man;
Man and maid did he make them.

Then God looked over all that he had made,
and it was excellent in every way . . . .
Genesis 1:27, 31 Living Bible

1

The First Step:

Affirming the Wonderful

Congratulations!

For what?

For the wonderful in you. No matter what you think, it's there. Still there. No way you could have erased it completely. God made you "excellent in every way."

Right now, can you put aside all your negatives to zero in on the plus?

Let's begin with a question: When was the last time you surprised yourself with a top quality performance? You felt a sense of pride in what you'd done. Honest pride. Or you were stirred with a genuine sympathy. You took time to listen, to feel, to help. You extended yourself, went out of your way to be kind.

Suddenly, you realized this was something fine you did.

Then there was that recent experience when temptation came and you stood your ground. You said *no* before you were swept along with the crowd. You took a stand. It wasn't the popular thing, but you heard a special call and responded. You championed a cause, defended someone, followed an inner light. And when it was over, you felt good about you.

So we begin with a pat on the back from you to you.

Sure there are some negatives around here. But there are some

real positives too. And to get the full picture we start way back
at the beginning:

> You are a part of God's creation—
> And "God made man like his Maker."

This is the day which the Lord hath made; we
will rejoice and be glad in it.

Psalms 118:24

2

Step Two:

Re-Tracking the Mind

Some days

> I am negative
> You are negative
> He is negative
> They are negative
> The whole sorry world is negative.
>> So where have all the flowers gone?

Before the Bible is one chapter old, it says:

God saw every thing that he had made, and, behold, it was very good.

What happened?
One answer is that God gave man free choice. Which was very nice of God really. Except that man sometimes deliberately went against God. Adam ate the apple and blamed it on Eve. I eat pie a la mode when I know I shouldn't. Plus chocolate cake. But Adam and I aren't the only ones. Christians believe there is only one exception to this rule, "All have sinned and come short of the

glory of God." That's an awesome answer to where have all the flowers gone. And it's basic.

Another answer is that we grew up in a background heavy on the downbeat. Radio, newspaper, magazine, television, telephone, table conversation:

"Mr. Brown is running around. And who would have thought *that?*"

"Seems like you can't trust anyone anymore."

"Stocks are down. Way down. Guess we'll all go broke if they keep going down."

"Isn't it awful? Aunt Margie has cancer."

Now push it further back:

"Don't get your feet wet. You might catch cold."

"You'd better stop that or mother won't like you."

Accidents. Illness. Gossip. Gloom. Sin.

Then even on Sunday, the awful news, "God is sure to get you if you don't watch out."

Psychologists say what we learned early is with us forever. Yet this is another part of the Good News. We *can* break the drag of the minus, and turn life into a plus.

This will take time. Hours, days, weeks, months, maybe all the days of one school year. I know it can happen, because it happened to me in seventh grade. Every morning Miss Wood would come bouncing into the room singing,

> Today is the day we give babies away,
> And with each a pair of new shoes.

She was a happy little redhead. Big smile. Gleam in her eye. Lights from way down inside.

First time I heard her sing it, I remember musing, "What kind of funny farm did this come from?" Yet every morning there it was again, coming on strong, "Today is the day . . . ."

And this was *my* year. The year of the good stuff. First team. A best friend. That fun poetry. Girls. Even mathematics broke through a little. Not much, but enough. So did Edgar Allan Poe and geography with its faraway places. Plus I could hardly believe all those fascinating new places close up through the microscope.

I wonder how much of my exciting seventh-grade world could be traced to the jolly little optimist? No doubt about it, she'd never do for adults. But for this seventh grader, she was some kind of special. A new note. New hope. "Life can be wonderful, Charlie! Today is the day!"

Awesome how one phrase can stay with us forever. Longer than anyone knew, it kept playing its record over. On the football field. Exam time. Dramatics. Debate. Summer vacations. Hours in the woods. My first job at the grocery store. And when I went away to college, the song played on:

> Today is the day we give babies away,
> And with each a pair of new shoes.

Sure, it was a frivolous little ditty, and not much to go on. But then again what if you were a boy growing up with nothing but put-down all around?

Then one day in college, I came on something similar from the Psalms. Could this be? Straight from the Lord? Same song. New verse.

Did Miss Wood know something I didn't know in seventh grade? Was she only getting us ready for the real thing? *God is the source of this day and all things good. Including the good in you and me.*

Beautiful news! Rejoice and be glad.

> If you can accept the fact that God made you . . . .
> If you can believe there really are some wonderful
>   things in you because He put them there . . . .

Then you are ready for the next important step. This is to "sound track" your mind with a new song.

Suggestion:

For thirty days, then sixty, ninety, repeat these words of the psalmist.

Every morning when you get up. Every evening. And frequently during the day run them through your mind. Play the record over and over. Let them become the new song in your soul.

This is the day which the Lord hath made; we will rejoice and be glad in it.

And I will restore to you the years that the locust hath eaten . . . .

Joel 2:25

3

Step Three:

Accepting the New Start God Offers Us

Susan has been riding up and down the West Coast in a Volkswagen bus. With friends. A miscellaneous assortment of other girls like Susan, plus a motley array of boys. They call themselves "the beautiful people." They "turn on." They turn on with drugs, alcohol, sex.

But lately Susan is turning off to all this. She's beginning to feel jaded, used, down on herself.

Dave has met up with something he can't handle. And that's a new feeling for Dave. He's been a roaring success. Clever, ingenious, a supersalesman. Somehow it seems everything Dave touches turns to dollars. In the eyes of all his friends (and in his own eyes), he's been "Mr. Big."

So with all this glamor, what kind of problems could Dave have?

To which comes the somber answer—Dave is beginning to wonder about Dave. Currently the problem is his second marriage. He left so much for this woman. First wife, three children, the respect of certain friends. Then there was that hurt look in his father's eye.

Dave was so sure he had found something lasting in this new

relationship. But some way it's never quite come off. Is this one, too, beginning to come unglued? The other night when they'd had a few too many, she said maybe she wanted out, wanted her share. Sure, she's backtracking now—saying she didn't mean it. *Did she?*

So maybe you could make a third million, but you still wouldn't like what you see in the mirror.

Most of us have a little bit of Susan and Dave inside—or a lot. Along with our pride in the good, there's the lurking shame for other things we've done. What about those times when we were less than our best? We cheated. We said one thing, meant another. We told half-truths, put somebody down, cut someone up. We stilled the inner voices, adjourned our principles, proceeded on our own selfish way.

Perhaps there is another reason we're not all we'd like to be. Maybe the people who shaped us made some serious mistakes. In order to defend ourselves from them, we compounded the problem by making bad choices.

Now what can we do with all of these negatives? How can we handle the not-so-good?

Psychiatry says *analyze.* Study your past. Locate the source of your neurotic trends. That's good. But is it good enough?

The answer is *no.* For some of us, inner research won't do it alone. Laying it all out for an honest look does not bring total healing. We need help for getting it together.

When we admit that need, we are ready for Step Three.

In Step One we affirm the wonderful of God's original creation.

In Step Two we adopt a program for re-tracking the mind—upward.

In Step Three *we accept the new start God offers us.* We aren't so wonderful anymore and we know it. But God is. That's the Good News.

Jesus came to tell us our Heavenly Father is like the father of Luke 15. Every day he goes out looking. Clear to the end of his lane he goes. This is no waiting father, arms folded, glowering.

He runs to meet the prodigal and our Heavenly Father runs to meet us.

The Los Angeles *Times* (classified section, PERSONALS) carried an interesting ad. It said simply:

I CAN FORGIVE WHAT YOU'VE DONE, SYLVIA. HONEST. YOU'LL ALWAYS BE WONDERFUL TO ME. PLEASE COME HOME.

This is the Gospel in one classified ad. It is God's ad for you, me, everyone of us. He cares so much for us that He welcomes us in His love. And in His love, He can restore the Divine creation in us.

Locusts in our crops? So?

What can we do?

Lord, thank You that You are also the Great Exterminator! Cleanse me that I may be all the wonderful things You had in mind for me. For You!

. . . Christ is all, and in all.
Colossians 3:11

4

Transcendental Meditation:

What Is It?

Transcendental Meditation is big these days. Its leaders say this is the fastest growing youth movement in the world. And they could be right. Dozens, hundreds, thousands are joining up.

I know they are, because I'm invited frequently to college campuses. So I have a close-up look at the goings-on. And when I discovered how big TM has become, I decided to research it for myself.

Transcendental Meditation is an ancient practice going far back into history. It is especially strong in Eastern countries, and in recent years TM has come on strong here.

Devotees are not limited to the college set. They can be found among housewives, businessmen, teachers, engineers, salesgirls, athletes. Doctors, lawyers, and other professional people have found it helpful.

The purpose of Transcendental Meditation is best explained from the ads:

Transcendental Meditation will:

- BRING YOU TO SELF-REALIZATION
- ACTIVATE YOUR CREATIVE INTELLIGENCE
- RELEASE POTENTIAL ENERGY
- TRANSCEND WORRY
- RESTORE PEACE

As I talked with these folks and attended their lectures, I made an interesting discovery. I was already into something similar and had been for twenty years.

It's simply super to be married to a woman who shares your prayer life with you. Long back, my Martha and I decided we'd make a pilgrimage together. We'd go down every possible road looking for authentic answers to prayer. We'd take new roads, old roads, and carve some out ourselves. One of these latter we call *Word Focusing.*

Word Focusing is a meditational approach which concentrates on a single word. As I listened to the TM people, I sensed this similarity. The student of TM is given a *mantra.* TM defines the *mantra* as a "sound, the effects of which are known." This mantra is a secret not to be shared.

As he begins to meditate the student thinks his mantra. It has a calming effect. Soothing. Without concentration, without effort, without worry, the meditator allows free flow of his thoughts.

Looking in from the outside, some will call this strange—queer —odd. But those who have talked much with the Transcendental Meditator will hear other sounds. These are the positive voices of those who have found it helpful. Here are some exact quotes from the college scene:

"I don't think TM changed me. Instead it allowed me to get a handle on some good things I didn't know I had."

"I feel more alive. I can think better, get more done. Yet at the same time I'm more relaxed."

"I can take other people better. They don't bug me so much anymore. It's like I can even appreciate them in a new way."

"They say it's great for your blood pressure. You know what I mean? Well, I'm not sure about that, but I just know I feel better all over."

These are straight from young people I know. Some I know well, like Ruth Helen. When she came into TM, she was very much on the lower levels. Emotionally, way down. Quarreling with her parents. Struggling to make her grades. Most of the time she was acting ugly, and all the time looking that way. She was also giving too much of herself to too many. Label her negative. Today Ruth Helen is moving up. Poised, inwardly quiet. Actually somewhat attractive.

And here's Terry. Terry was a "weirdo." That's what his family called him and he was doing little to refute their judgment. Much of the time he was totally out of it. Drugs. Mostly the milder stuff —but sometimes otherwise. Constantly tripping. Gradually disintegrating, and leaving pieces of himself wherever he'd been. Yet today if you could know Terry, I think you'd say, "Give him a plus." And if you'd known him before, you'd probably ask, "What happened?" Terry would give you the answer: Transcendental Meditation.

Lance credits TM with turning his grades around, from failing to passing. He's hoping now to make law school.

I could also tell you about Elizabeth, Jimmy, Robert, Mary Ann. All friends of mine—nice people. Some religious, some not. Then there is Bruce. I like what happened to him. Bruce had been completely turned off to the church and to the Lord. But today after eighteen months in Transcendental Meditation, he has returned to the Christian faith.

Transcendental Meditation denies that it is a religious movement. It is true that the roots of TM are from ancient Eastern mystics. However, the practice of TM today requires no religious beliefs, no denominational connection, no particular of philosophy. TM calls itself a *technique* with this purpose:

. . . to unfold the full potential of mind and heart and to live a life of freedom, fulfillment and happiness. Transcendental Meditation enables the student to experience directly the source of creative intelligence within himself and to apply it to all aspects of his life. (From *Transcendental*

Meditation: Maharishi Mahesh Yogi and the Science of Creative Intelligence, Jack Forem, E. P. Dutton & Co., Inc. 1973)

The Christian meditator also believes there is a source of creative intelligence within him. He calls this the *Inner Christ.* Claiming the biblical promise that "Christ is all and in all," * he seeks a personal relationship with the Divine. Now his prayer of prayers is:

Lord, bring me to my full potential. For my own fulfillment. For my effect on others. For Your purposes.

---

* (Moffatt translates this verse from Colossians 3:11, "Christ is everything and everywhere." Ronald Knox, in his version, goes even further with, "There is nothing but Christ in any of us.")

I exhort therefore, that, first of all, supplications, prayers, intercessions, and giving of thanks, be made for all men.

1 Timothy 2:1

5

Prayer:

"First of all . . . ."

There are twelve gates to the Holy City, and that's good. Most of us like a choice. We also like to pray in our own way—which is no doubt exactly the way God means it.

As far back as the Bible, men and women have been praying in an infinite variety of approaches. Children, too. Standing up, lying down, on their knees. Heads bowed, looking up, eyes open, eyes closed. Arms outstretched, hands folded. In crowds, in solitude. In temple, home, quiet grove, and noisy street corner. Rooftop. Inner chamber. Early morning, high noon, and the dark of night.

So it seems clear that any way we can pray, has to be good. Anytime. Anyplace. If we come sincerely, God meets us there.

For me, prayer has always gone best with a prayer partner. I believe man can pray by himself, and I do. I know from experience he can communicate with God, one on One. But for some of us a duet of prayer beats going it alone. And I'm one of these. There are also limitless options for prayer with others. But it's a fortunate man who can develop a prayer duo with the woman he loves.

When Martha and I started on our pilgrimage of prayer twenty years ago, we made a commitment. We would join hearts to discover if prayer could be real for us. We would read, research, discuss, ponder. We would write down our thoughts, try new things, experiment. We would pray alone and with each other. We decided to give it the time, the effort, the research until we knew the answer—is prayer real, and is it for us?

We have tried many things. Some described by others contributed zero to our lives. That's all right. It may even be very good. Nobody has all the answers. And this too comes through loud and clear. When we begin to think we're in a class by ourselves, the Bible tells us we're on dangerous ground. Some wag has said, "You can always tell a sophomore, but you can't tell him much." We have learned to be wary of sophomores at prayer who tell us we should have it exactly like they have it.

For us, every time we learned something new, we found something new to be learned. When we climb some exciting new hill, we see many more hills off in the distance, beckoning. Yet, isn't this one of the most thrilling aspects of prayer? Each discovery promises more to be discovered. So in our pilgrimage we have come to thank God for what we know. But that's not all. We have also learned to thank Him for what we don't know yet.

Here's one thing we have learned for sure—prayer is a discipline. For long-range growth, the haphazard won't do. This is true because of the myriad interruptions which threaten every one of us. For the smallest child and the oldest grandparent, life becomes cluttered. There are lessons to study, phones to answer, friends to tell us what they need to tell us. And then there are picky little details. Take Fido to the vet. Remember the junior-high game, and don't forget piano practice. Committee meetings, social engagements, church affairs. Get those crops planted. Group things, private things, things personal. These all tend to draw us away from the life of prayer.

Wouldn't it be superb if we could find some method for keeping the Lord in first place? The Quakers call it "centering down."

Today's young people talk about "turning on." We like "tune in." And that's what Word Focusing does for us. It helps us

Center down
Turn on
Tune in

. . . if therefore thine eye be single, thy whole body shall be full of light.

Matthew 6:22

6

"Singling the Eye"

In our study of prayer we learned about a group who called themselves Contemplatives. They lived far back in the Middle Ages with those mystics who wrote so well on prayer. Some of them apparently grouped themselves in monastic orders. They spent their time concentrating on things spiritual.

Their procedure? They would take a single phrase and repeat it constantly:

"My Lord and my God"

"Thou art my all in all."

"Praise His Holy Name"

"In Him is our peace"

These and countless other phrases opened up new roads to God for them. That's what they claimed, and we believe their claim. We believe it, because we tried it and it worked for us.

Then another wonderful thing happened. The more we practiced contemplation, the more we found that phrases could be much too much. Sometimes a single word would put us in touch with The Inner Presence.

So we're grateful to the Contemplatives (whoever they were, wherever, and when) for doing their thing so well and reporting it. We may also learn more in the future from today's Contemplatives.

Jesus used the interesting phrase "single eye" in Matthew 6:22. He said if we could single our eye, this would make a mighty difference. In us. To us. Through us.

That's what we are about with Word Focusing. We are singling the mind's eye on one quality of God:

Courage
Hope
Health
Love
Balance
Fervor
Control

No believer would argue that God is everyone of these. He is all of these and more. Yet here is an even greater fact about the nature of God: He wants to share His nature with us. Word Focusing is built on this premise—the God who created us longs to express Himself through us.

In order to accomplish this, He created our minds so that they are manageable. When we make the effort, we *can* follow one train of thought. It *is* possible to choose one subject for concentration.

Most of us will not find this easy. We will need to crack down hard on our concentrator. And nowhere is this firm grip more essential than in our prayer life. Unless we mean business, meditation becomes a kind of skittering here and skittering there. We kneel to pray and a screech of tires sets our mind flying:

We must get the brakes checked. Saturday . . . . Saturday is also for mowing . . . . Gas for the mower. Don't forget . . . . Did I make a note of that appointment? . . . Why didn't I write that letter? . . . All the resulting criticism could have been avoided if only I'd written that letter!

So we set out praying and here we are moping over a letter. To which a chorus of echoes, "*Amen.* Me too. Seriatim and *in extenso.*"

What can we do about this willy-nilly dancing in our heads?

The best thing we've found for mind control is Word Focusing. By this method we have taught ourselves to single our eye on one attribute of God. Word Focusing sorts out other thoughts for the moment. It continually calls our mind back from its flitting. And the more we practice it, the more we can feel the distractions go. We experience integration.

Some time ago I was in an airport making a phone call. At the phone next to me an old man—very old—was looking through the directory. Only he wasn't looking like I would look. And not like most people. Instead he had rolled up a piece of paper shaping it like a funnel. He pointed the narrow end right down to the page, then peered through the larger opening. Watching me watching him, he smiled and said, "Ever try it, son? Sometimes when you cut out all the other print, you can see what you're looking for real plain."

That "looking real plain" and "singling the eye" is what Word Focusing has done for us.

. . . the kingdom of God is within you.

Luke 17:21

7

The How of Getting Through to the Wonderful You

WANTED TO BUY

Special kind of house. Prefer at least one acre with trees. Two-story older home suitable for remodeling. Would like basement, attic, fireplace, hardwood floors, brick exterior. If yours meets this description, and you will sell, write:

Box 100, The Evening Press

He wrote the ad at his office and carried it home for his wife's approval. But as he was sharing it with her, he suddenly came to an abrupt stop with, "You know, Maude, this sounds a whole lot like the house we're living in."

Most of us are prone to think what we want is somewhere else. We scan the scenery, we peer behind this fence, hunt down those roads, search the terrain.

But Jesus said this isn't the way. People of His day were looking for the Kingdom in desert, sanctuary, secret chambers. Some lifting their eyes to the hills said, "See—there it is." Others were asking, "When will it begin?" "Do I go to the housetops to look for it?" "If I build bigger barns, stack my assets higher, buy more land, will I find it then? Let us eat, drink, and be merry! Maybe we will discover the secrets in our revelling."

To which came the surprising reply: Life's deepest satisfactions are an inside job. "The kingdom of God is within you."

So Christian meditation, as described here, is *not an effort to empty the mind.* It rather clears the mind to control it. And even this is not the full purpose of Christian meditation. *The full purpose is to activate The Inner Presence.* God made us. He indwells us. When we believe that and want to live by that belief, we are ready to begin.

I like the old preacher's description of his preaching:

> "First, I tell them what I'm going to tell them.
> Next I tell them.
> Then I tell them what I've told them and send
>   them on their way."

Thanks for the idea, whoever you were. It does make things easy to remember. So I tell you now what I'm going to tell you. This is the *how* of Word Focusing:

We begin by selecting a word.

Then we look up our word in the dictionary.

We set aside a regular time for meditating on our word, and we retain this word until it has done its thing in us.

Now let's backtrack, and I'm going to tell you what I told you.

Suppose our word is *patience.* One morning in our quiet time it leaps out at us when we're reading in the New Testament. (Words don't always step right out of the Bible to demand our attention. That being the case, sometimes we choose a word and find it in Scripture. For this approach a concordance may be useful. The Christian meditator will also find it helpful to pray about his word choice.)

But this morning, you see the right word immediately. There it is: "For ye have need of patience . . ." (Hebrews 10:36). How right can You be, Lord! We need it badly. So we write down the verse on a slip where we can refer to it often. Eventually the slip gives way to our memory. We know it by heart.

Now comes a very important mental maneuver. It is so easy to begin our praying at the wrong place.

"Lord, I'm getting impatient with my children . . . . That woman at the next desk. I don't think I can stand her much longer . . . . How can my boss possibly be so stupid?"

And so on far into the day. You sense immediately what is happening: We are not meditating now on *patience,* but on *impatience.*

"Heavenly Father, help me put up with all these people" is one kind of prayer. But it isn't the best. The best is to begin with Him. And if our need is patience, the finest kind of prayer starts with His patience.

Next we turn to the dictionary. In Funk and Wagnalls we find this definition:

Patient 1. Possessing or demonstrating quiet, uncomplaining endurance under distress or annoyance; long-suffering. 2. Tolerant, tender, and forbearing. 3. Capable of tranquilly awaiting results.

The use of several dictionaries can be a genuine plus for Word Focusing. It isn't true that a dictionary is a dictionary. Different dictionaries were put together by different people with different slants. Sometimes their meanings are identical. But frequently interpretations vary enough that the second dictionary opens new windows. Then as we meditate, we feel fresh breezes through the curtains.

Having pondered the Bible verse and seen it through the light of several dictionaries, we now make this word a focal point of our meditating.

Patience—Lord, if I could only wait five minutes longer. There is this eager beaver in my soul pushing to make the rose bloom right now. How can a small heart like mine hold enough patience for all these big and little problems?

Answer: "It can't. But Christ living in you can."

With myself—with the events of my life—I need the infinite long-suffering which only comes when the Lord of love rules my heart.

How long do we keep the word *patience?* Sometimes we change our words daily. Maybe we keep the word two days—three days— a week. Or if it continues opening up new insights, we may retain it several weeks.

Some words come alive suddenly. Some don't. Some are usable again and again. Now and then a word which didn't do much for us the first time, really gets up to move on our second try.

All this is no panacea. We still lose our cool, blow our stack, say things we shouldn't say. What do we do? One thing we do is to quit beating ourselves. Our meditation on His patience has brought us more patience with ourselves. So with our human frailties, knowing that He knows, we turn again in His direction. Only a little move of the mind and soul, and we feel something wonderful—He brings His patience to us. Word Focusing has led us to the place where we can say:

> Lord, I don't have all the answers.
> But I know where the answers are.
> Thank You for Your patience.
> Fill the gaps in my patience with Your patience.

This then is the procedure:
- Select a word
- Study its meaning
- Meditate

You are on your way.

Evening, and morning, and at noon, will I
pray . . . .

Psalms 55:17

8

Finding Time for the Quiet Time

Transcendental Meditation asks its followers to set aside two periods daily. Twenty morning minutes. Twenty minutes later in the day.

Word Focusing goes better for us when we begin the day with a quiet time. During this period we read, we meditate, we listen. We try to relate our mind to the mind of God and tune our spirit to His Spirit.

For us, it is almost uncanny how our faithfulness to the morning quiet affects the quality of each day. We had a bad day? Did we hurry through our morning quiet time? Or was this a day when it seemed the birds were singing just for us? Didn't their lovely song this day start in our moments of meditation?

One of my friends says, "I don't hardly believe in God before 8:30 in the morning." Morning meditation wouldn't do for him.

Another slow starter has his meditation immediately after lunch. He closes the door, tells his secretary he has an important appointment and meditates. (She knows what he's doing.) Of course, he has to make exceptions. But he says there is no exception here—this is his best time.

Still another meditates at night in his bed before he sleeps. That's great for him, but I'd be long gone before I made it to the first level.

"To each his own." Does it really matter when? Probably not. What matters is that we make a commitment. So whether we choose morning, evening, noon, or some other hour, here is another plus in Word Focusing:

We are able to tune in quickly.

at the red light
when someone keeps us waiting
moments of temptation
when the phone rings
a knock at the door
the sudden need
tension
anger
worry
high times
good news
bad news
disappointments

In these pockets of time we can use our word to reconnect with the Infinite.

But let no one suppose this form of meditation is a casual meandering up to God as the day passes. This is a discipline. Say it again loud and clear: *Meditation is for getting in touch with The Inner Presence.* We meditate that He might be our Lord, our Controller, Chairman of the Board.

Sometimes our meditation is plain hard work. Why wouldn't it be? Jesus said, "Strive to enter in at the strait gate . . ." (Luke 13:24). He made it clear that it takes all there is of us to be all He wants us to be.

The psalmist does a good thing when he commits himself to prayer morning, evening, and at noon. Repetition is the key to many skills.

Practice. Practice. Practice.
Steady staying with it.

Do it again. And again. And again.

> He who prays well prays much.
> And he who prays much
> At last becomes a living prayer.
> Almost.

How precious it is, Lord, to realize that you
are thinking about me constantly!
Psalms 139:17 Living Bible

9

Different Strokes:

How Others Get in Touch With God

Different strokes
For different folks

It's a catchy little couplet which comes on strong when we grasp its full meaning. God, in His wisdom, made each of us unique. And that's good. But here's something even better:

The God who made us didn't go off and leave us. He follows us, He looks for openings. And when we provide them, He moves in.

I personally believe Transcendental Meditation is effective with some people for this reason. Even when they do not call His Name, He follows them. Through their quiet, they may be providing Him an opening.

As we have developed Word Focusing for ourselves, we have taught it to others. Fantastic, the variety.

Helen is the mother of Hughie, Alice Ann, and then came Donald. Probably nobody but the parent of a hyperactive child would know the full meaning of that term. Because Doug travels, the problem leans heaviest on Helen. Donald requires constant care.

Quote from a mother's soul:

"I just don't think I could make it without my meditation. Of course, I knew God cared, but I had to have some way to get in touch with Him. Some of the words I've used have made all the difference between sanity and going completely out of my mind. One of my favorites is *control*. It's simply great to know that I can actually draw on God's control when mine runs out. When you have to be a programmer, and an eagle eye, plus a referee, you need help almost every minute, and sometimes you need help fast."

How does she do it? One of her methods is to write her current word on slips of paper. Then she posts these at strategic places. The refrigerator door. Bathroom mirror. By the telephone, in Donald's room, and above her kitchen sink.

Jennifer is a real student of Word Focusing. She's been developing her techniques for several years. So we asked her to write some suggestions on how she does it. One paragraph from her answer deals with the handling of difficult people.

You know what a struggle I've had in the past with Jerry's business partner. Unfortunately, we're still thrown with them too much. And his wife isn't any improvement on him. I wonder what I did before I learned to meditate! Right now my word is *compassion*. I ponder the compassion of Christ and ask Him to activate His compassion in me. It is absolutely unbelievable how much difference this makes. When she calls on the phone, I repeat the word. And do you know what I think? I think you can learn to meditate in a flash— like making contact in seconds. Recently, Jerry asked me to teach him, too. Isn't that wonderful?

Logan is a corporation lawyer. Most of his time is spent on contracts. He's a dedicated man of prayer. We meet for lunch frequently. From one of our conversations I selected these words (used by permission):

"I love my job, but I always run scared. I miss one little item and it could cost a bundle. Might even affect the whole future of our company. You ask how Word Focusing helps me. Well, I go big for words like *comprehension, light, wisdom.* I use them driving to work on the freeway. Then I turn to them again as I begin work on a contract. When I come on an option, a choice I have to make, I may even pause long enough to ask for Divine light, for wisdom greater than my own."

Another of our closest friends is a leading surgeon. He's a regular in our prayer group.

This is his witness:

"Before each operation I like to get alone for a few minutes and meditate. One of my best words is *preparation.* I like the feeling that God is already preparing for the needs of the patient. What I mean is, I'm trying to prepare myself for His preparation. It's really great for me and I know it helps."

Suzanne is a high-school junior. Very popular.

"You wouldn't believe how much certain words help on my dates. To know you can get in touch with the Lord any moment you need Him is simply super.

"You asked for some of my favorite words. Well, this may sound strange, but one I especially like is *closeness.* Sometimes I need that. Especially with this one neat guy. When I'm getting too excited, *closeness* helps me remember who I really want to be close to."

Dave is a cross-country runner. He set a new conference record this year. And if you could talk with him, he'd tell you one reason is his practice of Word Focusing. *Energy* is one of his favorites.

Some of the most successful reports from Word Focusing come out of groups. Almost every conceivable combination, mind to mind and heart to heart can profit by united prayer. Bible-study cells, Sunday-school classes, choirs, committees, the church staff, relatives, friends, business partners.

And perhaps the most exciting group reports come from family units.

Straight from where a miracle is taking place, a college boy writes:

My mom and dad have never been very big on the Bible. I guess they prayed. But we didn't pray together. Then my sister and I started them on this word thing. They really caught on. As a matter of fact, they got with it so much, our whole family does it together and it's absolutely the greatest.

Moment for praise—

The God who made us individuals also attends our celebration with each other!

Say it again and again and again. Then say it one more time: Word Focusing works because it opens doors for the God who is constantly thinking of us. As the psalmist says, that is a precious realization!

Call to me and I will answer you, and will tell you great and hidden things . . . .
Jeremiah 33:3 Revised Standard Version

10

Results and Rewards of Word Focusing

One year at Christmas we were given a strange gift. It came from two of our dearest friends. But it looked more like some kind of put-on.

When we opened the box, there carefully wrapped, was a dried-up plant. Brown and brittle leaves, gray stems, dirt on the bulb. What could it be? "Thanks for nothing."

But the company which sold it to our friends must have known how it would appear at first sight. So they included a card which read:

PLEASE DON'T THROW ME AWAY.
I REALLY AM A BEAUTIFUL "STAR OF BETHLEHEM!"
PUT ME IN A DARK PLACE, WATER ME, AND WAIT.

We did. And some time later, the miracle.
The instructions also read:

WHEN I BEGIN TO GET GREEN, BRING ME INTO THE LIGHT. YOU WILL BE SURPRISED.

That is exactly how it happened. What looked so dead came alive with green, yellow, white, and touches of blue. Fascinating.

Away at the center all that time some dormant beauty had been stirring. No one could see, but it was there. *No one?* Not quite. The God of the flowers was doing His work beneath the surface. Slow, steady, quiet, little by little.

For most Christians, maturity will not come SPECIAL DELIVERY tomorrow. We can accept Christ in a moment. In one cataclysmic happening we can see the light, hear His call, and respond. But there are not many among us who would say, "Look at me. I am a full-grown Christian." And should it be our misfortune to meet one of these, we sense a kind of delusion. When Jesus said, "Be ye therefore perfect . . ." (Matthew 5:48), He threw out a challenge to last us forever. Little by little we grow. Days, weeks, months, years. All these it will take to answer His call *en toto*.

It's in the Book—staying with it is the secret of secrets. The promises of God are "true and righteous altogether" (Psalms 19:9). But they may not be speedy! We should have known. Jesus told us they wouldn't come in a rush. Same song, next verse. "He that *endures* to the end shall be saved" (*see* Matthew 10:22, 24:13).

What can Word Focusing accomplish? Physically, mentally, spiritually, what can it do for us?

Nobody knows for sure all the sources of his strength. But two people we know well can report these wonders taking place inside them. Over the years. Slowly. We have felt these effects in our bodies.

> There is a new sense of aliveness
> We have more energy
>   Vibrancy
>   Faster healing
> We move easier
>   We're coordinated
>   Exercise is more fun
> We eat better
> We sleep more soundly
> We experience sex at its finest

All this brings us a new respect for our body. Nerves. Muscles. Cells. Fibers. "Leg bone connected to the knee bone." Often comes the awesome realization that God is at work in every one of these. No way we could prove it. No way to explain it. But we can feel it.

For most of us, the mind works better when the body is at its best. Mental progress may be harder to docket than physical improvement. But this, too, is real for us.

> We have new powers of concentration
>> Better judgment
>> More accurate recall
> We can think through many ramifications
>> Sense the true
>> See the false
> We sharpen our originality
>> Liberate the locked-up
>> Surprise ourselves with good ideas
> We become more efficient
>> Organize intelligently
>> Accomplish more at a slower pace

Makes sense, doesn't it? The more we use our mind in meditation, the more our mind comes alive for purposes which matter. Higher purposes. His.

We're thankful for every indication that good things are happening in our body. We thrill to every sign of improvement in our ability to think up to our best. But good as these are, there is one thing better: This is the sure knowledge that we are growing spiritually.

We know we haven't arrived, but we do feel the certain unfolding of good things inside us.

We are more tolerant with a healthy tolerance.

We can take a new attitude toward other people, their idiosyncrasies, and our own.

We experience grace for ourselves, and we have a new ability
    to forgive.
We have more strength to handle criticism,
    deal more kindly with the ugly, hear their cry.
    We can be more gentle.
    There is a new flexibility about us.
When we make a mistake we know what to do with it.
    We can accept true guilt.
    We can put false guilt where it belongs.
    Fears go.
Hounding perfectionism gives way.
    We can be glad now that others do things better than we do
      them.
    Jealousy subsides.
    We can love.
    We find new courage to be ourselves.
    We feel an honest pride in the things we do.
    The things we make take on more beauty, more meaning.
We can trust.
    Trust ourselves
    Trust others
    Trust the Lord
All this brings true joy.
    Lasting joy
    Peace
    The seasons of pure peace come more frequently
    They last longer
Then is there any higher gift than this?

We experience true gratitude!

It says here:

"Call to me and I will answer you and will tell you great and
hidden things."

        This is His promise.
        Yet He doesn't say when.

Since a thousand years are as a day in His sight, we may hear Him saying:

> *Stay with it*
> *Hang in there*
> *You be faithful, and I will.*

For it was by him that all things were created
. . . . and all coheres in him.

Colossians 1:16, 17 Moffatt

11

Mr. Pettit's Memorable Experiment

Mr. Pettit was our high-school science teacher. And his course wasn't my thing. But years later I still remember some of his experiments.

One day he went up and down the aisles putting a paper on every desk. A white sheet. Blank. Next he poured a pile of steel shavings on each paper. When he had finished, he said, "Spread the shavings out now. Your problem for today is to bring them all back into a cluster. Without touching."

Some of us decided we'd blow them back. With lung power like ours, no way! They only scattered.

Others tried burning their paper. No go here, either. Some of the shavings were too heavy. These wouldn't budge, while lighter ones fell to the floor.

Finally, one girl came up with the answer. She went to the cabinet, took out a magnet, held it over her shavings and drew them together.

Mr. Pettit must have known what would happen. His theme for the day (typically Pettit):

COHERENCE FROM INTRODUCTION OF GREATER POWER TO LESSER POWER

Which to this high-schooler meant simply: When you can't get it all together, you've got to have help from somewhere.

Beautiful translation, Moffatt: ". . . all coheres in him."

Another scholar puts it: "In and through Him the universe is one harmonious whole."

That is good news. But there is even better news.

We ourselves can be one harmonious whole when we let *Him* draw us together.

Appendix 1

Words, Words, Words

Words, words, thousands of words. Old words. New words. And more new words coming on.

I have one writer friend who says there should be a law prohibiting new words. He gives me the feeling we are about to be buried under an avalanche. Personally, I like it. More words make the world of words more interesting. New words also give us more new ways to praise the Lord.

Words presented here are chosen because they have been helpful to us in Word Focusing.

Section A contains words and the Scripture verse where we found them. With these we include some dictionary meanings. The prayers, affirmations, questions, represent thoughts which come to us as we meditate.

Section B drops added thoughts, leaving these for the individual. This section presents only words, Bible verse, dictionary meanings.

In *Section C* we list additional words with Bible reference only.

In *Section D* we leave a page (for starters!) for your own favorite Scripture verses in Word Focusing.

Section A

Getting Started With:

Words, Definitions, Prayers, Affirmations, Questions

One dictionary on our shelves boasts more than forty-five thousand vocabulary entries (it's a small dictionary). Some scholars say that with variations, this can be blown up ten times. Most of us will settle for the first number. But this is one side-happening from our Word Focusing—excitement from the discovery of the new, the old, and fresh meanings to both. Section A presents key words we have found helpful in our meditation. These are listed in alphabetical order.

Key to dictionary symbols:

(F&W) *Funk & Wagnalls Standard College Dictionary*
(WCD) *Webster's New Collegiate Dictionary*
(RHD) *Random House Dictionary of the English Language*

ABUNDANCE

And God is able to provide you with every blessing in abundance, so that you may always have enough of everything and may provide in abundance for every good work.

2 Corinthians 9:8 RSV

abundance 1: an ample quantity . . . 3: relative degree of plentifulness . . . (WCD)

PRAYER

Lord, why do I fuss so much about Your goodness
    running out before it gets to me?
Why do I worry that I may be shortchanged
    Or miss my share of treasures
        from Your storehouse?
Have I been straining for *things* instead of
    reaching for *You?*
Help me to exchange my poverty complex
    for an abundance complex.
Teach me to move my eyes from intake to outgo—
    I know it is true and I want to remember:
    When I give what I should,
    You provide what I need.
But that isn't all.
    When I live in this truth,
    You can provide what other people
        need through me.
Write it on my heart:
    You are the Lord of "ample quantity,
        plentifulness."
And I am Your trustee.

THOUGHT FOR THE DAY

I hold in my hand this large draft on the goodness
   of God.
He will honor it at the right time in the right way—
When He knows I am in right relationship with Him.

CLOSENESS

I keep the Eternal at all times before me; with him so close, I cannot fail.

Psalms 16:8 MOFFATT

---

close   26. being in or having proximity in space or time . . . 28. near, or near together, in a kind of relationship . . . 30. based on a strong uniting feeling of respect, honor, or love . . . (RHD)

How I am doing in my spiritual development can be measured by this question: Are the periods of intimate feeling between me and my Lord increasing?

This is an awesome thought. God is interested in everything I do. Big deal, minor matters, every hour, all the minutes. "Sorry to bother You, Lord" never needs to be said. My Heavenly Father's theme is, "No bother, ever. Bring it to Me."

Every person on earth needs at least one close friend. Close enough to listen. Close enough to care. Close enough to share the big things, the little. God would like to be this kind of friend.

Jesus came to give us this idea of God, and to make His friendship real. When I believe this, my prayer life takes on tremendous new dimensions. I begin to understand the scope of prayer, its many facets, many forms. I try them all with new meaning—the prayer of petition when I do the talking—I ask. The prayer of conversation when both talk—dialogue. The listening prayer when I still myself and hear what He has to say—silence. Neither of us says one thing. There is nothing more to say. This is it. This is the full communion of holy oneness for which Christ came and for which I was created.

"With him so close, I cannot fail."

CONTROL

For the love of Christ controls us . . . .
2 Corinthians 5:14 RSV

Control 1. To exercise a directing, regulatory or governing influence over. 2. To restrain, curb. (F&W)

I saw a huge Saint Bernard dog remain poised in the heat of a frenzied attack. "Large One" sat on the curb and a tiny Pekingese yapped furiously to drive him away. But Mr. Big only blinked his great eyes and waited in full composure. Those heavy jowls! Ominous! One snap to consume the enemy! But they didn't open. True saint. Total self-government. Perfect restraint. Absolute control.

I can learn much from this king of the canine gentry. I need such curbing and checking for my own life.

But to the Christian, self-control is really not self-control at all. Perfect Christian control is Christ-control.

Steady me, Lord, by Your restraint.
Check me. Direct me. Control me.

Drop Thy still dews of quietness,
Till all our strivings cease;
Take from our souls the strain and stress,
And let our ordered lives confess
The beauty of Thy peace. *Amen.*

JOHN GREENLEAF WHITTIER

ENLARGEMENT

I will run in the way of thy commandments when thou enlargest my understanding!

Psalms 119:32 RSV

---

enlarge 1: to make larger: EXTEND 2: to give greater scope to: EXPAND (WCD)

Wise counselor to his patient: "Go up on a mountain. Take a plane ride. Anything to get a broader view. Your trouble is you can't see beyond your own troubles. This is a big world—but you don't know it."

Too often I sit tight on my isolated island. I settle in for too long a stay. Meanwhile, out there a whole range of new experience waits for my discovery. My soul draws little circles about bits of truth. I wall myself in. I peer furtively over the edge. Would I dare risk a wider orbit?

Spiritually speaking, I need to follow the Christ in me to new horizons. Outward. Upward.

Jesus has no limits. Whenever I give Him free play in my soul, He increases its capacity. He stretches out the heart for more of Himself.

My prayer life is only what it should be if I am becoming a bigger person in His bigness.

Question:

Am I expanding in my relationship with the Lord? Am I running from Him? Toward Him? With Him? Is my way His Way— the Way of His Commandments?

GLADNESS

Serve the Lord with gladness . . . .
Psalms 100:2

---

glad 2a: experiencing pleasure, joy, or delight: made happy 4: full of
brightness and cheerfulness (WCD)

In his prologue to the New Testament, 1525, William Tyndale
wrote that the Gospel is:

Good, merry, glad and joyful tydings, that maketh a mannes
hert glad, and maketh hym synge, daunce, and leep for joye.

This I need. Recently, I had a period when my heart was
especially alive. Life was better than it had been in a long time.

Why not now? Same ingredients here today—me, my job,
friends, a healthy mind, food, clothing, the Bible, forgiveness,
love.

One of my saintly friends reminds me, "Happiness may depend
on what happens to you. Christian joy runs through whatever
happens."

Happy Hour: 5:00–7:30

Lord, I have this sad feeling when I see that sign. Lounge. Bar.
Motel marquee. Artificial gladness. Phony fun. Heavy hearts.
Looking for someone to care. Spending their money for joy
where it isn't.

Prayer:
Help me to remember where the real thing is. And whenever
my joy goes away, teach me this too: You haven't left. I have.

INFLUENCE

A wise man is esteemed for being pleasant; his friendly words add to his influence.

Proverbs 16:21 MOFFATT

---

influence 2: an emanation of spiritual or moral force 3a: the act or power of producing an effect without apparent exertion of force . . . (WCD)

The writer of Proverbs here opens a two-way road.

Those things I see, the voices I hear, the thoughts I entertain —these will affect me. They influence me. Then having done that, they influence others. My words, my acts, my touch—these make my influence on other lives.

Prayer:

Lord, I can hardly believe it—
I am a part of Your influence.
But today I spoke too quickly—
Or I didn't speak.
I failed to take that stand—
     Forgive me.
Help me to remember that others are reading You by
     reading me.
Filter the forces flowing into my life that I may be a better
     influence for You.

MATURITY

Therefore let us leave the elementary doctrine of Christ and go on to maturity. . . .

Hebrews 6:1 RSV

Mature   2. Highly developed or advanced in intellect, moral qualities, outlook . . . 3. Fully or thoroughly developed, perfected, detailed . . . (F&W)

Prayer:

>   Lord, do you need me on a higher plane?
>   Teach me to open my mind for fresh thoughts.
>   Grow me up.
>   Expand my understanding.

Check questions for frequent review:
   1. Can I tell the important from the unimportant?
   2. Do I have the wisdom to keep silent when I should?
   3. Is it easier for me to apologize when I am wrong?
   4. Do I have the courage to stand for what I believe?
   5. Am I increasingly able to pray for those who do not like me?
   6. Do I have less desire to strike back?
   7. Are my reading habits—my thoughts—continually moving up to higher levels?

Question to answer all questions:

>   Am I going on when Christ calls?

SIMPLICITY

The Lord preserveth the simple . . . .
Psalms 116:6

---

simple 1: free from guile: INNOCENT 2b: free from ostentation or display 3: of humble origin or modest position 9: readily understood or performed (WCD)

Prayer for simplicity in my work—

Here is my schedule, Lord.
     Things seem so complicated—
     Am I reading You right?
     These are my complications—not Yours!
Could I simplify by leaving more of the work to other people?
Or if I dropped the ostentations, would that make it easier?
Down there in the control room where You and I do business,
    teach me to be straightforward;
Lord, when I try to be too pensive,
     Show me that mighty truths can be made plain
     If I work hard enough to make them plain.
Help me to be my natural self. The one You made me to be:
    Simply Yours.

For thinking through:

The way to become profound is to develop an inner simplicity with Christ.

SINCERITY

Now therefore fear the Lord, and serve him in sincerity and in faithfulness . . . .

Joshua 24:14 RSV

Sincerity Honesty of purpose or character; freedom from hypocrisy, deceit, or simulation. (F&W)
sincere 2: marked by genuineness: TRUE (WCD)

This word may have come from two Latin words *sine* (without) and *cērā* (wax). Buying Roman crocks and vases was risky business. Some had been waxed over to hide their blemishes. Yet who am I to point the finger? Am I everything I appear to be?

Basic question.

From Old Testament time, today, and forever, God wants His followers genuine.

My prayer life can never be fully effective so long as there are "simulations," "deceits," "hypocrisies." Yet God never forces me.

So long as I insist on faking it, He lets me.

Prayer:

> Such a rude guest You are, Lord.
> You insist on seeing every room.
> You open every closet door, look under every rug,
> unlock every file.
> Help me to understand You only want to share Your
> Presence fully.
> I hamper You badly when I insist You behave like
> a visitor.
> Come. Take over.
> I am only sincere when You are my "all in all."

TRANQUILITY

Well, my very first counsel is that supplications, prayers, petitions, and thanksgiving, are to be offered for all men—for kings and all in authority, that we may lead a quiet, tranquil life in all godliness and gravity. It is good to pray thus, it is acceptable to our Saviour.

1 Timothy 2:1–3 MOFFATT

---

tranquility   . . . calmness; peacefulness; . . . serenity. (RHD)

Mothers, fathers, businessmen—
Sales force, salesladies, traveling salesmen—
Public workers, postal clerks, policemen—
Lawyers, doctors, pastors, leaders—
　　Same problem.

The more our heart becomes a boulevard for traffic of many kinds, the more we must build our private props. Unless we do this, we are asking for nervous collapse, physical collapse, moral collapse, total collapse.

First Timothy 2:1–3 says that prayer should produce a quiet, tranquil life.

When I rush about looking for peace outside myself, I can know my prayer life is defective. Praying right and praying much will produce deep serenity within.

Regardless of the conditions without, regardless of the invasions on my privacy, regardless of the interruptions, prayer produces quiet.

There is a grade school of prayer when I talk to God. There is an advanced school when I allow Him to talk to me. Then there is the graduate level of "togetherness" which needs no words. How do I reach that level? By putting my life at one with Christ. This is a state of pure tranquility, and it is acceptable to Him.

Thought for the day:
　　The purest retreat is retreat into the heart of God.

Section B

Words, Bible Verses, Dictionary Meanings

Here the meditator will find it helpful to create his own prayers, questions, affirmations to meet particular needs.

ASSURANCE

And the work of righteousness shall be peace; and the effect of righteousness quietness and assurance for ever.

Isaiah 32:17

Assurance 2. A positive statement, intended to give confidence, encouragement, etc. 3. Firmness of mind . . . certainty. (F&W)

ATTRACTIVENESS

Finally, brothers, keep in mind . . . whatever is attractive . . . .

Philippians 4:8 MOFFATT

Attractive Having the quality of attracting interest or affection; pleasing; winning. (F&W)

CHEERFULNESS

Having gifts that differ according to the grace given to us, let us use them . . . . he who gives aid, with zeal; he who does acts of mercy, with cheerfulness.

Romans 12:6, 7 RSV

cheerful 1a: full of good spirits: MERRY b: UNGRUDGING 2: . . . likely to dispel gloom or worry (WCD)

1. In good spirits; joyous; lively. 3. Willing . . . (F&W)

101

COMPASSION

Finally, be ye all of one mind, having compassion one of another, love as brethren . . . .

1 Peter 3:8

---

compassion: 1. a feeling of deep sympathy and sorrow for another who is stricken by suffering or misfortune . . . (RHD)

Pity for the suffering or distress of another, with desire to help or to spare. (F&W)

COMPREHENSION

For this reason I bow my knees before the Father, from whom every family in heaven and on earth is named, that according to the riches of his glory he may grant you to be strengthened with might through his Spirit in the inner man, and that Christ may dwell in your hearts through faith; that you, being rooted and grounded in love, may have power to comprehend with all the saints what is the breadth and length and height and depth, and to know the love of Christ which surpasses knowledge, that you may be filled with all the fulness of God.

Ephesians 3:14–19 RSV

---

comprehension: 5. perception or understanding. 6. capacity of the mind to perceive and understand; power to grasp ideas; ability to know. (RHD)

CONTENTMENT

. . . I have learned, in whatsoever state I am, therewith to be content.

Philippians 4:11

Content Freedom from worry . . . ease of mind; satisfaction. (F&W)

COURAGE

Then you will prosper if you are careful to observe the statutes and the ordinances which the Lord commanded Moses for Israel. Be strong, and of good courage. Fear not; be not dismayed.

1 Chronicles 22:13 RSV

courage: 1. the quality of mind or spirit that enables one to face difficulty, danger, pain with firmness and without fear; bravery. 3. have the courage of one's convictions, to act in accordance with one's beliefs . . . (RHD)

COURTESY

Finally, be ye all of one mind, having compassion one of another, love as brethren . . . be courteous.

1 Peter 3:8

courtesy 1b: a courteous act or expression 2b: consideration, cooperation, and generosity in providing . . . (WCD)

DILIGENCE

The lazy man finds life beset with thorns; the diligent finds it a well-paved road.

Proverbs 15:19 MOFFATT

diligence 2: persevering application: ASSIDUITY (WCD)

2. Proper heed; care. (F&W)

DISCIPLINE

My son, do not regard lightly the discipline of the Lord . . . .
Hebrews 12:5 RSV

---

discipline: 1. training to act in accordance with rules . . . 2. instruction and exercise designed to train to proper conduct or action . . . (RHD)

ENTRY

So be the more eager, brothers, to ratify your calling and election, for as you exercise these qualities you will never make a slip; you will thus be richly furnished with the right of entry into the eternal realm of our Lord and saviour Jesus Christ.
2 Peter 1:10, 11 MOFFATT

Entry   1. The act of coming or going in; entrance. (F&W)

EXAMPLE

. . . but I received mercy for this reason, that in me . . . Jesus Christ might display his perfect patience for an example to those who were to believe in him for eternal life.
1 Timothy 1:16 RSV

---

example   2: one that serves as a pattern to be imitated . . . (WCD)

GENEROSITY

. . . be kind to each other, be tender-hearted, be generous to each other as God has been generous to you in Christ.

Ephesians 4:32 MOFFATT

generosity 1a: liberality in spirit or act (WCD)
generous 2a: . . . MAGNANIMOUS, KINDLY 2b: liberal in giving: OPEN-HANDED (WCD)

HEALTH

Never pride yourself on your own wisdom, revere the Eternal and draw back from sin: that will mean health for your body and fresh life to your frame.

Proverbs 3:7, 8 MOFFATT

health 1a: condition of being sound in body, mind, or spirit . . . (WCD)

HONESTY

Shun evil and do good, so shall you live your life within the land; for the Eternal, who loves honesty, never forsakes his faithful band.

Psalms 37:27, 28 MOFFATT

honesty: 1. . . . uprightness . . . integrity. 2. truthfulness, sincerity, or frankness. 3. freedom from deceit or fraud. Syn. 1. fairness, justice . . . 2. candor . . . (RHD)

HOPE

And now, Lord, what wait I for? my hope is in thee.
Psalms 39:7

hope 1: to cherish a desire with expectation of fulfillment 2b: someone or something on which hopes are centered . . . (WCD)

6. to believe, desire or trust. 7. to feel that something desired may happen . . . (RHD)

1. Desire accompanied by expectation . . . 3. That which is desired or anticipated . . . (F&W)

INTELLIGENCE

And I have filled him with the Spirit of God, with ability and intelligence . . . .
Exodus 31:3 RSV

Intelligence 1. The faculty of perceiving and comprehending meaning; mental quickness; active intellect; understanding. 2. The ability to adapt to new situations, and to learn from experience. 3. The inherent ability to seize the essential factors of a complex matter. (F&W)

LIGHT

Then Jesus again addressed them, saying, "I am the light of the world: he who follows me will never walk in darkness, he will enjoy the light of life."
John 8:12 MOFFATT

Light 1. The form of radiant energy that stimulates the organs of sight . . . 2. The condition or medium that makes vision possible; illumination . . . not dark. (F&W)

LOVE

Love is very patient, very kind. Love knows no jealousy; love makes no parade, gives itself no airs, is never rude, never selfish, never irritated, never resentful; love is never glad when others go wrong, love is gladdened by goodness, always slow to expose, always eager to believe the best, always hopeful, always patient. Love never disappears.

1 Corinthians 13:4–8 MOFFATT

---

love: 1. the profoundly tender or passionate affection for a person of the opposite sex. 2. a feeling of warm, personal attachment or deep affection, as for a parent, child, or friend . . . 4. A person toward whom love is felt . . . (RHD)

OBEDIENCE

. . . obedience to God's commands is everything . . . .

1 Corinthians 7:19 MOFFATT

---

obedient submissive to the restraint or command of authority (WCD)

2. Deferring habitually to laws, superiors . . . (F&W)

OPPORTUNITY

As we have therefore opportunity, let us do good unto all men . . . .

Galatians 6:10

---

opportunity a favorable juncture of circumstances . . . (WCD)

1. an appropriate or favorable time or occasion. (RHD)

ORDER

The steps of a good man are ordered by the Lord: and he delighteth in his way.

Psalms 37:23

order 5b: a regular or harmonious arrangement; 6a: the customary mode of procedure . . . (WCD)

PERFECTION

Be ye therefore perfect, even as your Father which is in heaven is perfect.

Matthew 5:48

perfection: 2. the highest degree of proficiency . . . 3. a perfect embodiment of something. 4. a quality, trait, or feature of the highest degree of excellence. 5. the highest or more perfect degree of a quality or trait. (RHD)

POWER

For God did not give us a spirit of timidity but a spirit of power and love and self-control.

2 Timothy 1:7 RSV

Power 1. Ability to act; capability. 2. Potential capacity. 9. Any form of energy available for doing work . . . (F&W)

PRAISE

Let my mouth be filled with thy praise and with thy honour all the day.

Psalms 71:8

Praise verb—1. To express approval and commendation of; applaud; eulogize. 2. To express adoration of, glorify . . . noun—The glorifying and honoring of a god, ruler, hero . . . especially, worship of God expressed in song. (F&W)

1. the act of expressing approval or admiration; commendation; laudation. 2. the offering of grateful homage in words or song, as an act of worship . . . 3. state of being approved or admired . . . (RHD)

RADIANCE

If you will turn your mind to God and stretch your hands to him . . . your life will rise more radiant than the moon, your shadows will be like the dawn.

Job 11:13, 17 MOFFATT

---

radiant 2: marked by or expressive of love, confidence, or happiness (WCD)

REFRESHMENT

Repent ye therefore, and be converted, that your sins may be blotted out, when the times of refreshing shall come from the presence of the Lord.

Acts 3:19

Refreshment . . . 1. Restoration of vigor or liveliness. (F&W)

refresh 1: to restore strength and animation to: REVIVE 2: freshen up: RENOVATE (WCD)

RENEWAL

*Do not be conformed to this world but be transformed by the
renewal of your mind, that you may prove what is the will of
God, what is good and acceptable and perfect.*

Romans 12:2 RSV

Renew 1. To make new or as if new again . . . 6. To revive; reestablish.
(F&W)

SAFETY

*And you will have confidence, because there is hope; you will
be protected and take your rest in safety.*

Job 11:18 RSV

---

safety: 1. state of being safe; freedom from . . . injury, danger, or loss.
(RHD)
safe: (Synonym Study) . . . applied . . . to a person or thing that is out
of, or has passed beyond, the reach of danger . . . (RHD)

SERENITY

*He is like a tree planted beside a stream, reaching its roots to
the water; untouched by any fear of scorching heat, its leaves are
ever green, it goes on bearing fruit in days of drought, and lives
serene.*

Jeremiah 17:8 MOFFATT

---

serene 1b: shining bright and steady . . . 2: marked by or suggestive of
utter calm . . . (WCD)

SILENCE

The Eternal is good to those who wait for him, to a soul that seeks him. It is good to wait in silence for the help of the Eternal.

Lamentations 3:25, 26 MOFFATT

silence: 1. absence of any sound or noise; stillness. 7 . . . quiet. (RHD)

STEADINESS

He has no fear of evil tidings, he trusts the Eternal with a steady heart.

Psalms 112:7 MOFFATT

Steady 2. Moving or acting with uniform regularity; constant; unfaltering . . . 3. Not readily disturbed or upset . . . 4. . . . reliable. (F&W)

STRENGTH

On the day I called, thou didst answer me, my strength of soul thou didst increase.

Psalms 138:3 RSV

Strength 1. . . . being strong; muscular force or power. 2. . . . solidity; tenacity; toughness. 3. Power in general, or a source in power. (F&W)

TRUST

Blessed is that man that maketh the Lord his trust . . . .
Psalms 40:4

---

trust 1a: to commit, or place in one's care or keeping: ENTRUST 2b: to place confidence in: rely on 2c: to hope or expect confidently (WCD)

USEFULNESS

If any one purifies himself from what is ignoble, then he will be a vessel for noble use, consecrated and useful to the master of the house, ready for any good work.
2 Timothy 2:21 RSV

---

useful capable of being put to use: SERVICEABLE; *esp:* having utility (WCD)

Section C
Words With Texts

Springboards for the quiet time. Words and texts only. The student of Word Focusing can add to these indefinitely, keeping his own log, making his own discoveries.

Adoration	Isaiah 12:1, 2 (MOFFATT)
Attentiveness	Deuteronomy 15:5 (MOFFATT)
Calm	Mark 4:39
Commitment	Psalms 37:5
Dependence	Colossians 3:17 (MOFFATT)
Discernment	1 Kings 3:9
Ease	Proverbs 1:33 (RSV)
Expectancy	Psalms 62:5
Friendship	John 15:14 (RSV)
Harmony	Romans 12:16–18 (MOFFATT)
Hospitality	1 Peter 4:9
Inheritance	Psalms 106:4, 5
Justice	Job 37:23
Kindness	Proverbs 21:21 (RSV)
Laughter	Psalms 126:1–3
Liveliness	1 Peter 1:3
Loveliness	Philippians 4:8
Nearness	Psalms 46:1 (MOFFATT)
Persistence	Luke 11:8–10 (MOFFATT)
Purpose	Psalms 33:11 (MOFFATT)
Readiness	2 Corinthians 8:12 (RSV)
Renunciation	2 Corinthians 4:1, 2 (RSV)
Sanctification	2 Timothy 2:19–21
Success	Joshua 1:7, 8 (RSV)
Supply	Philippians 4:19
Thanksgiving	Psalms 100:4
Transference	Colossians 1:11–13 (MOFFATT)
Zeal	Romans 12:11 (RSV)

Section D

List Your Favorite Scripture Verses for Word Focusing

Appendix 2

Frequent Queries on Word Focusing

Questions and Answers

There have been many encouraging signs on the church scene in our time. One of these is development of groups for spiritual growth. Invited often to conventions, seminars, conferences, Martha and I have shared Word Focusing with many. In our presentations we find that dialogue is always more productive than monologue. So we have a period when people share their ideas, ask questions, and discuss. Following are some of the most frequent queries.

Family Devotions

QUESTION

You mentioned Word Focusing as a help to family devotions. We've tried almost everything. Bible reading, sentence prayers, books. But we just can't seem to keep it going. Life gets so frantic at our house. And mealtimes are no exception. Know what I mean?

ANSWER

Yes, I do know what you mean. So do most parents. And this is one reason why Word Focusing can be a winner. It provides a place for coalescing. No matter what type family devotions you have, this can be an interesting supplement.

When the whole group has decided together what word to use, each one can meditate on it individually and then share ideas. Anything you can do to keep the tribe communicating has to be good. At our house, *celebration* is the key to an effective family altar. And if it's going to last, it better be fun. (Those wishing more detailed description of our fun family devotions are referred to *Promises to Peter,* Charlie Shedd, Word, Inc. 1970, and *Fun Family Forum* cassette series, Word 1975, "The Fun Family Devotions" FFT-010.)

Group Word Focusing

QUESTION

Would you tell us a little more about the use of Word Focusing in groups? Bible Study groups? Prayer groups?

ANSWER

Our groups have practiced Word Focusing as a supplement to other studies. Words are selected by the group and used individually until their next meeting. Then when they come together, they share their insights.

Some of them talk between sessions. They support each other. Meet special needs. Relate their findings. Over coffee. On the phone.

In this way Word Focusing contributes to the feeling of togetherness. It adds variety as it makes for oneness.

Wool-gathering

QUESTION

Why do you think it's important to focus your mind on one thought? What's the matter with letting it wander?

ANSWER

Nothing the matter with letting the mind wander. Sometimes. "Wool-gathering" can be fun. So is fantasizing—within limits. But if we let our thoughts go with no direction, we may not accomplish what the Lord wants from us. Then, too, without some kind of inner control, the mind turns in a downward direction. Check it out. If you're like the rest of us, mental drag is a real threat. Without some counteraction, our thoughts become negative. We concentrate on the bad news. We mull over mistakes we've made. Trot out old worries. Feel sorry for ourselves. Mope.

Word Focusing at its best provides a spiritual upward thrust.

Dangers of Overcommunicating

QUESTION

A psychiatrist once told me you need to be careful not to over-communicate. What he meant was you could share too much of yourself too soon. Do you think Word Focusing might lead to this danger?

ANSWER

Your psychiatrist is right. When we begin to reveal the hidden places of our heart, we better be sure what we're doing. Shaping our words and feelings requires time. We feel, however, that Word Focusing has its own built-in protection. Remember, we're moving toward Christ control. If this is authentic, He shows us what to reveal.

A far greater danger is that we are not sharing what we should be sharing. This may be particularly true at home. We wall ourselves off. Husbands hide from wives and wives from husbands. Children clam up. Teenagers barricade themselves. The result is a kind of chronic loneliness.

Word Focusing can be a big assist in keeping the bridges cleared between us and other people. It tells us what to reveal. When. How. It gives us the courage to open up. As we experience the love of Christ in our hearts, we are freed to express our total selves in the right way.

TM—A Substitute for Religion

QUESTION

I've heard the Transcendental Meditation people recently set a goal to get everyone in the world meditating. I don't think there's much chance of that happening. But if they did, do you think it would become a substitute for religion?

ANSWER

Like you, I don't see it happening soon. But there are some items we should note here.

Say it one more time: Transcendental Meditation is *not* a religion. Neither is it antireligious. The word used often in TM is *technique.*

You are right about this. Theirs is a gigantic aim. A mammoth challenge thrown out by their leaders.

This would be an excellent goal for any good movement. But Christians know this is not original with TM. Jesus said, "Go ye into all the world and make disciples of all nations." (*See* Matthew 28:19.)

The Work of Satan?

QUESTION

What do you think about the charges that Transcendental Meditation is the tool of the devil and the work of Satan? There are people who say that TM is a sinister force which comes to us out of a non-Christian background. These same folks claim that if it isn't halted, it will destroy Christianity. If that is true, shouldn't we all join forces and take a firm stand against it?

ANSWER

Most of the people I know who are into TM accept it as a technique, not a religion. Ask them. The vast majority of these folks couldn't care less about TM's ancient history and its original sources. They are after results now. Even if all these negative charges were true, I believe there is only one way to counteract evil—this is with something better, and the Christian says there is nothing better than the inner life with Christ developed to its maximum.

Selecting a Bible

QUESTION

Do you recommend one Bible over others for use in Word Focusing? With so many translations I get confused. How do we know they are all authentic?

ANSWER

It is confusing. There is a veritable blizzard of versions coming at us. Translations, too. Some scholars say a version may be more dependable than a translation. The reason? A translation usually means one scholar did the work himself. Versions are the work of several minds pooling their skills.

Whether or not that is true, I think it's great to have so many choices. And I'm sure God is perfectly capable of defending Himself against a few inaccuracies.

Collecting different renditions makes an interesting hobby. More than thirty versions and translations are available in the bookstores and from Bible sellers. Almost every one of these has something going for it. You will have your favorites. I have mine. But I don't think anyone of us can go far wrong with any Bible which speaks to us personally.

Word Focusing—Boring to Others

QUESTION

Couldn't all this talk about Word Focusing be a bore to other people—like members of the family? Sometimes at our house they give me the impression, "Ho-hum, Mom is on another religious kick."

ANSWER

When we get excited about the Lord, it's good to gauge our enthusiasm by potential response. I'm interested in those times when Jesus said nothing. Was it because anything He might say would turn His hearers off? We know families who are into Word Focusing together. And they tell us it's been a great thing in their home.

At a recent family conference where we were discussing meditation, a high-school girl said:

"You wouldn't believe the difference in my mother since she started this meditation thing. She used to be so nervous and crabby all the time. Now you can actually talk to her about some things without her getting mad."

Is there any finer witness than a life tuned in to the Lord?

TM—Just Another Kick

QUESTION

Why this sudden interest in Transcendental Meditation? I understand it's about four thousand years old. Do you think this is just a kick, or will it last?

ANSWER

Maybe it surfaces now to meet a deep underlying need. I have a theory that the rise of TM is attributable in no small part to the church. In almost every denomination there has been a tragic dearth of prayer emphasis. In some of our standard denominations, ministers are suspect of anything which smacks of piety. This is too bad, but it is understandable. There are some very strange movements purporting to be the real thing.

So what's the answer? The answer is a sensible prayer program developed with particular application for daily living. Wherever you find a minister who dares lead in this kind of prayer effort, you will find a turned-on congregation.

I know a number of churches which now feature a fellowship where every member is prayed for every day by someone. (See *The Exciting Church—Where People Really Pray*, Charlie Shedd,

Word, Inc. 1975.) Jesus said He wanted His church to be a house of prayer. I have a feeling the church of the future will focus more on spiritual growth.

Husbands and Wives— Meditating Together

QUESTION

You talk about husbands and wives praying together. Would you give us a little more on this? When you use Word Focusing, do you meditate together? Frankly, our schedule is the kind where some days we hardly even see each other. What about us?

ANSWER

You are right on target to a basic problem in many homes. And this is one of the reasons why Word Focusing has been such a blessing with us. We find it a powerful magnet drawing us to each other. Sometimes we meditate in duet. More often we meditate individually. During the day when we're apart, our word gives us a feeling of togetherness. But no matter how we do it, we like the results—a melding of these two souls into oneness with the Lord.

A young wife says, "The thing we like about Word Focusing is that this is the only method of prayer we're comfortable with. What I mean is, we have tried other things, but they seem awkward. We get embarrassed. But with this we are actually having some fun. It seems to give us a place for coming together. Yet it also allows us to respect each other's privacy."

The Positive Emphasis of Word Focusing

QUESTION

All this talk about the positive makes me a little nervous. Aren't you de-emphasizing the hard part of Christianity? Sin, the devil, judgment? Evil is real in our world too, isn't it?

ANSWER

You bet, it's real. And not just in the world. It's also real in me. So you're right. We should never sidestep the negative.

But here's the key question: What is the *major* emphasis of my life?

I think right here our basic theology is all-important. Do I believe the first chapter of Genesis or don't I? Is man created in the image of God? Am I? Are you? If that is an irrevocable part of our doctrine, then "getting through to the wonderful you" is an irrevocable part of our call.

I'm a sinner. I hope you might consider that you could be. But that's not the Good News. Jesus came to tell us that God's love is stronger than man's sin. Do I believe this, or don't I? If I do, then I must not become morbid about the evil around me or in me. Instead I must dedicate all my spiritual energy to activating The Inner Presence.

For us this is the true positive.

Goal straight from the Book

"PRAY WITHOUT CEASING"
1 Thessalonians 5:17

Lord, teach me to meditate so well
That I may live constantly in
   touch with You.
This day is Your day.
Today may I be so much in tune
That my life is a living prayer.

Index of Words for Word Focusing